Tartuffe

by Moliere

By

Jean Baptiste Poquelin de Moliere

Table of Contents

Introduction

Jean Baptiste Poquelin, better known by his stage name of Moliere, stands without a rival at the head of French comedy. Born at Paris in January, 1622, where his father held a position in the royal household, he was educated at the Jesuit College de Clermont, and for some time studied law, which he soon abandoned for the stage. His life was spent in Paris and in the provinces, acting, directing performances, managing theaters, and writing plays. He had his share of applause from the king and from the public; but the satire in his comedies made him many enemies, and he was the object of the most venomous attacks and the most impossible slanders. Nor did he find much solace at home; for he married unfortunately, and the unhappiness that followed increased the bitterness that public hostility had brought into his life. On February 17, 1673, while acting in "La Malade Imaginaire," the last of his masterpieces, he was seized with illness and died a few hours later.

The first of the greater works of Moliere was "Les Precieuses Ridicules," produced in 1659. In this brilliant piece Moliere lifted French comedy to a new level and gave it a new purpose—the satirizing of contemporary manners and affectations by frank portrayal and criticism. In the great plays that followed, "The School for Husbands" and "The School for Wives," "The Misanthrope" and "The Hypocrite" (Tartuffe), "The Miser" and "The Hypochondriac," "The Learned Ladies," "The Doctor in Spite of Himself," "The Citizen Turned Gentleman," and many others, he exposed mercilessly one after another the vices and foibles of the day.

His characteristic qualities are nowhere better exhibited than in "Tartuffe." Compared with such characterization as Shakespeare's, Moliere's method of portraying life may seem to be lacking in complexity; but it is precisely the simplicity with which creations like Tartuffe embody the weakness or vice they represent that has given them their place as universally recognized types of human nature.

Characters

MADAME PERNELLE, mother of Orgon
ORGON, husband of Elmire
ELMIRE, wife of Orgon
DAMIS, son of Orgon
MARIANE, daughter of Orgon, in love with Valere
CLEANTE, brother-in-law of Orgon
TARTUFFE, a hypocrite
DORINE, Mariane's maid
M. LOYAL, a bailiff A Police Officer
FLIPOTTE, Madame Pernelle's servant

Act 1

Scene 1

The Scene is at Paris

MADAME PERNELLE and FLIPOTTE, her servant; ELMIRE, MARIANE, CLEANTE, DAMIS, DORINE

MADAME PERNELLE Come, come, Flipotte, and let me get away.

ELMIRE You hurry so, I hardly can attend you.

MADAME PERNELLE Then don't, my daughter-in law. Stay where you are. I can dispense with your polite attentions.

ELMIRE We're only paying what is due you, mother. Why must you go away in such a hurry?

MADAME PERNELLE Because I can't endure your carryings-on, And no one takes the slightest pains to please me. I leave your house, I tell you, quite disgusted; You do the opposite of my instructions; You've no respect for anything; each one Must have his say; it's perfect pandemonium.

DORINE If ...

MADAME PERNELLE You're a servant wench, my girl, and much Too full of gab, and too impertinent And free with your advice on all occasions.

DAMIS But ...

MADAME PERNELLE You're a fool, my boy—f, o, o, l Just spells your name. Let grandma tell you that I've said a hundred times to my poor son, Your father, that you'd never come to good Or give him anything but plague and torment.

MARIANE I think ...

8

MADAME PERNELLE O dearie me, his little sister! You're all demureness, butter wouldn't melt In your mouth, one would think to look at you. Still waters, though, they say ... you know the proverb; And I don't like your doings on the sly.

ELMIRE But, mother ...

MADAME PERNELLE Daughter, by your leave, your conduct In everything is altogether wrong; You ought to set a good example for 'em; Their dear departed mother did much better. You are extravagant; and it offends me, To see you always decked out like a princess. A woman who would please her husband's eyes Alone, wants no such wealth of fineries.

CLEANTE But, madam, after all ...

MADAME PERNELLE Sir, as for you, The lady's brother, I esteem you highly, Love and respect you. But, sir, all the same, If I were in my son's, her husband's, place, I'd urgently entreat you not to come Within our doors. You preach a way of living That decent people cannot tolerate. I'm rather frank with you; but that's my way— I don't mince matters, when I mean a thing.

DAMIS Mr. Tartuffe, your friend, is mighty lucky ...

MADAME PERNELLE He is a holy man, and must be heeded; I can't endure, with any show of patience, To hear a scatterbrains like you attack him.

DAMIS What! Shall I let a bigot criticaster Come and usurp a tyrant's power here? And shall we never dare amuse ourselves Till this fine gentleman deigns to consent?

DORINE If we must hark to him, and heed his maxims, There's not a thing we do but what's a crime; He censures everything, this zealous carper.

MADAME PERNELLE And all he censures is well censured, too. He wants to guide you on the way to heaven; My son should train you all to love him well.

DAMIS No, madam, look you, nothing—not my father Nor anything—can make me tolerate him. I should belie my feelings not to say so. His actions rouse my wrath at every turn; And I foresee that there must come of it An open rupture with this sneaking scoundrel.

DORINE Besides, 'tis downright scandalous to see This unknown upstart master of the house— This vagabond, who hadn't, when he came, Shoes to his feet, or clothing worth six farthings, And who so far forgets his place, as now To censure everything, and rule the roost!

MADAME PERNELLE Eh! Mercy sakes alive! Things would go better If all were governed by his pious orders.

DORINE He passes for a saint in your opinion. In fact, he's nothing but a hypocrite.

MADAME PERNELLE Just listen to her tongue!

DORINE I wouldn't trust him, Nor yet his Lawrence, without bonds and surety.

MADAME PERNELLE I don't know what the servant's character May be; but I can guarantee the master A holy man. You hate him and reject him Because he tells home truths to all of you. 'Tis sin alone that moves his heart to anger, And heaven's interest is his only motive.

DORINE Of course. But why, especially of late, Can he let nobody come near the house? Is heaven offended at a civil call That he should make so great a fuss about it? I'll tell you, if you like, just what I think; (Pointing to Elmire) Upon my word, he's jealous of our mistress.

MADAME PERNELLE You hold your tongue, and think what you are saying. He's not alone in censuring these visits; The turmoil that attends your sort of people, Their carriages forever at the door, And all their noisy footmen, flocked together, Annoy the neighbourhood, and raise a scandal. I'd gladly think there's nothing really wrong; But it makes talk; and that's not as it should be.

CLEANTE Eh! madam, can you hope to keep folk's tongues From wagging? It would be a grievous thing If, for the fear of idle talk about us, We had to sacrifice our friends. No, no; Even if we could bring ourselves to do it, Think you that everyone would then be silenced? Against backbiting there is no defence So let us try to live in innocence, To silly tattle pay no heed at all, And leave the gossips free to vent their gall.

DORINE Our neighbour Daphne, and her little husband, Must be the ones who slander us, I'm thinking. Those whose own conduct's most ridiculous, Are always quickest to speak ill of others; They never fail to seize at once upon The slightest hint of any love affair, And spread the news of it with glee, and give it The character they'd have the world believe in. By others' actions, painted in their colours, They hope to justify their own; they think, In the false hope of some resemblance, either To make their own intrigues seem innocent, Or else to make their neighbours share the blame Which they are loaded with by everybody.

MADAME PERNELLE These arguments are nothing to the purpose. Orante, we all know, lives a perfect life; Her thoughts are all of heaven; and I have heard That she condemns the company you keep.

DORINE O admirable pattern! Virtuous dame! She lives the model of austerity; But age has brought this piety upon her, And she's a prude, now she can't help herself. As long as she could capture men's attentions She made the most of her advantages; But, now she sees her beauty vanishing, She wants to leave the world, that's leaving her, And in the specious veil of haughty virtue She'd hide the weakness of her worn-out charms. That is the way with all your old coquettes; They find it hard to see their lovers leave 'em; And thus abandoned, their forlorn estate Can find no occupation but a prude's. These pious dames, in their austerity, Must carp at everything, and pardon nothing. They loudly blame their neighbours' way of living, Not for religion's sake, but out of envy, Because they can't endure to see another Enjoy the pleasures age has weaned them from.

MADAME PERNELLE (to Elmire) There! That's the kind of rigmarole to please you, Daughter-in-law. One never has a chance To get a word in edgewise, at your house, Because this lady holds the floor all day; But none the less, I mean to have my say, too. I tell you that my son did nothing wiser In all his life, than take this godly man Into his household; heaven sent him here, In your great need, to make you all repent; For your salvation, you must hearken to him; He censures

11

nothing but deserves his censure. These visits, these assemblies, and these balls, Are all inventions of the evil spirit. You never hear a word of godliness At them—but idle cackle, nonsense, flimflam. Our neighbour often comes in for a share, The talk flies fast, and scandal fills the air; It makes a sober person's head go round, At these assemblies, just to hear the sound Of so much gab, with not a word to say; And as a learned man remarked one day Most aptly, 'tis the Tower of Babylon, Where all, beyond all limit, babble on. And just to tell you how this point came in ...

(To Cleante) So! Now the gentlemen must snicker, must he? Go find fools like yourself to make you laugh And don't ...

(To Elmire) Daughter, good-bye; not one word more. As for this house, I leave the half unsaid; But I shan't soon set foot in it again,

(Cuffing Flipotte) Come, you! What makes you dream and stand agape, Hussy! I'll warm your ears in proper shape! March, trollop, march!

Scene 2

CLEANTE, DORINE

CLEANTE I won't escort her down, For fear she might fall foul of me again; The good old lady ...

DORINE Bless us! What a pity She shouldn't hear the way you speak of her! She'd surely tell you you're too "good" by half, And that she's not so "old" as all that, neither!

CLEANTE How she got angry with us all for nothing! And how she seems possessed with her Tartuffe!

DORINE Her case is nothing, though, beside her son's! To see him, you would say he's ten times worse! His conduct in our late unpleasantness. Had won him much esteem, and proved his courage In service of his king; but now he's like A man besotted, since he's been so taken With this Tartuffe. He calls him brother, loves him A hundred times as much as mother, son, Daughter, and wife. He tells him all his secrets And lets him guide his acts, and rule his conscience. He fondles and embraces him; a sweetheart Could not, I think, be loved more tenderly; At table he must have the seat of honour, While with delight our master sees him eat As much as six men could; we must give up The choicest tidbits to him; if he belches, ('tis a servant speaking) Master exclaims: "God bless you!"— Oh, he dotes Upon him! he's his universe, his hero; He's lost in constant admiration, quotes him On all occasions, takes his trifling acts For wonders, and his words for oracles. The fellow knows his dupe, and makes the most on't, He fools him with a hundred masks of virtue, Gets money from him all the time by canting, And takes upon himself to carp at us. Even his silly coxcomb of a lackey Makes it his business to instruct us too; He comes with rolling eyes to preach at us, And throws away our ribbons, rouge, and patches. The wretch, the other day, tore up a kerchief That he had found, pressed in the Golden Legend, Calling it a horrid crime for us to mingle The devil's finery with holy things.

13

Scene 3

ELMIRE, MARIANE, DAMIS, CLEANTE, DORINE

ELMIRE (to Cleante) You're very lucky to have missed the speech She gave us at the door. I see my husband Is home again. He hasn't seen me yet, So I'll go up and wait till he comes in.

CLEANTE And I, to save time, will await him here; I'll merely say good-morning, and be gone.

Scene 4

CLEANTE, DAMIS, DORINE

DAMIS I wish you'd say a word to him about My sister's marriage; I suspect Tartuffe Opposes it, and puts my father up To all these wretched shifts. You know, besides, How nearly I'm concerned in it myself; If love unites my sister and Valere, I love his sister too; and if this marriage Were to ...

DORINE He's coming.

Scene 5

ORGON, CLEANTE, DORINE

ORGON Ah! Good morning, brother.

CLEANTE I was just going, but am glad to greet you. Things are not far advanced yet, in the country?

ORGON Dorine ...

(To Cleante) Just wait a bit, please, brother-in-law. Let me allay my first anxiety By asking news about the family.

(To Dorine) Has everything gone well these last two days? What's happening? And how is everybody?

DORINE Madam had fever, and a splitting headache Day before yesterday, all day and evening.

ORGON And how about Tartuffe?

DORINE Tartuffe? He's well; He's mighty well; stout, fat, fair, rosy-lipped.

ORGON Poor man!

DORINE At evening she had nausea And couldn't touch a single thing for supper, Her headache still was so severe.

ORGON And how About Tartuffe?

DORINE He supped alone, before her, And unctuously ate up two partridges, As well as half a leg o' mutton, deviled.

ORGON Poor man!

16

DORINE All night she couldn't get a wink Of sleep, the fever racked her so; and we Had to sit up with her till daylight.

ORGON How About Tartuffe?

DORINE Gently inclined to slumber, He left the table, went into his room, Got himself straight into a good warm bed, And slept quite undisturbed until next morning.

ORGON Poor man!

DORINE At last she let us all persuade her, And got up courage to be bled; and then She was relieved at once.

ORGON And how about Tartuffe?

DORINE He plucked up courage properly, Bravely entrenched his soul against all evils, And to replace the blood that she had lost, He drank at breakfast four huge draughts of wine.

ORGON Poor man!

DORINE So now they both are doing well; And I'll go straightway and inform my mistress How pleased you are at her recovery.

Scene 6

ORGON, CLEANTE

CLEANTE Brother, she ridicules you to your face; And I, though I don't want to make you angry, Must tell you candidly that she's quite right. Was such infatuation ever heard of? And can a man to-day have charms to make you Forget all else, relieve his poverty, Give him a home, and then ... ?

ORGON Stop there, good brother, You do not know the man you're speaking of.

CLEANTE Since you will have it so, I do not know him; But after all, to tell what sort of man He is ...

ORGON Dear brother, you'd be charmed to know him; Your raptures over him would have no end. He is a man ... who ... ah! ... in fact ...a man Whoever does his will, knows perfect peace, And counts the whole world else, as so much dung. His converse has transformed me quite; he weans My heart from every friendship, teaches me To have no love for anything on earth; And I could see my brother, children, mother, And wife, all die, and never care—a snap.

CLEANTE Your feelings are humane, I must say, brother!

ORGON Ah! If you'd seen him, as I saw him first, You would have loved him just as much as I. He came to church each day, with contrite mien, Kneeled, on both knees, right opposite my place, And drew the eyes of all the congregation, To watch the fervour of his prayers to heaven; With deep-drawn sighs and great ejaculations, He humbly kissed the earth at every moment; And when I left the church, he ran before me To give me holy water at the door. I learned his poverty, and who he was, By questioning his servant, who is like him, And gave him gifts; but in his modesty He always wanted to return a part. "It is too much," he'd say, "too much by half; I am not worthy of your pity." Then, When I refused to take it back, he'd go, Before my eyes, and give it to the poor. At length heaven bade me take him to my home, And since that day, all seems to

18

prosper here. He censures everything, and for my sake He even takes great interest in my wife; He lets me know who ogles her, and seems Six times as jealous as I am myself. You'd not believe how far his zeal can go: He calls himself a sinner just for trifles; The merest nothing is enough to shock him; So much so, that the other day I heard him Accuse himself for having, while at prayer, In too much anger caught and killed a flea.

CLEANTE Zounds, brother, you are mad, I think! Or else You're making sport of me, with such a speech. What are you driving at with all this nonsense ... ?

ORGON Brother, your language smacks of atheism; And I suspect your soul's a little tainted Therewith. I've preached to you a score of times That you'll draw down some judgment on your head.

CLEANTE That is the usual strain of all your kind; They must have every one as blind as they. They call you atheist if you have good eyes; And if you don't adore their vain grimaces, You've neither faith nor care for sacred things. No, no; such talk can't frighten me; I know What I am saying; heaven sees my heart. We're not the dupes of all your canting mummers; There are false heroes— and false devotees; And as true heroes never are the ones Who make much noise about their deeds of honour, Just so true devotees, whom we should follow, Are not the ones who make so much vain show. What! Will you find no difference between Hypocrisy and genuine devoutness? And will you treat them both alike, and pay The self-same honour both to masks and faces Set artifice beside sincerity, Confuse the semblance with reality, Esteem a phantom like a living person, And counterfeit as good as honest coin? Men, for the most part, are strange creatures, truly! You never find them keep the golden mean; The limits of good sense, too narrow for them, Must always be passed by, in each direction; They often spoil the noblest things, because They go too far, and push them to extremes. I merely say this by the way, good brother.

ORGON You are the sole expounder of the doctrine; Wisdom shall die with you, no doubt, good brother, You are the only wise, the sole enlightened, The oracle, the Cato, of our age. All men, compared to you, are downright fools.

CLEANTE I'm not the sole expounder of the doctrine, And wisdom shall not die with me, good brother. But this I know, though it be all my knowledge, That there's a difference 'twixt false and true. And as I find no kind of hero more To be admired than men of true religion, Nothing more noble or more beautiful Than is the holy zeal of true devoutness; Just so I think there's naught more odious Than whited sepulchres of outward unction, Those barefaced charlatans, those hireling zealots, Whose sacrilegious, treacherous pretence Deceives at will, and with impunity Makes mockery of all that men hold sacred; Men who, enslaved to selfish interests, Make trade and merchandise of godliness, And try to purchase influence and office With false eye-rollings and affected raptures; Those men, I say, who with uncommon zeal Seek their own fortunes on the road to heaven; Who, skilled in prayer, have always much to ask, And live at court to preach retirement; Who reconcile religion with their vices, Are quick to anger, vengeful, faithless, tricky, And, to destroy a man, will have the boldness To call their private grudge the cause of heaven; All the more dangerous, since in their anger They use against us weapons men revere, And since they make the world applaud their passion, And seek to stab us with a sacred sword. There are too many of this canting kind. Still, the sincere are easy to distinguish; And many splendid patterns may be found, In our own time, before our very eyes Look at Ariston, Periandre, Oronte, Alcidamas, Clitandre, and Polydore; No one denies their claim to true religion; Yet they're no braggadocios of virtue, They do not make insufferable display, And their religion's human, tractable; They are not always judging all our actions, They'd think such judgment savoured of presumption; And, leaving pride of words to other men, 'Tis by their deeds alone they censure ours. Evil appearances find little credit With them; they even incline to think the best Of others. No caballers, no intriguers, They mind the business of their own right living. They don't attack a sinner tooth and nail, For sin's the only object of their hatred; Nor are they over-zealous to attempt Far more in heaven's behalf than heaven would have 'em. That is my kind of man, that is true living, That is the pattern we should set ourselves. Your fellow was not fashioned on this model; You're quite sincere in boasting of his zeal; But you're deceived, I think, by false pretences.

ORGON My dear good brother-in-law, have you quite done?

CLEANTE Yes.

ORGON I'm your humble servant.

(Starts to go.)

CLEANTE Just a word. We'll drop that other subject. But you know Valere has had the promise of your daughter.

ORGON Yes.

CLEANTE You had named the happy day.

ORGON 'Tis true.

CLEANTE Then why put off the celebration of it?

ORGON I can't say.

CLEANTE Can you have some other plan In mind?

ORGON Perhaps.

CLEANTE You mean to break your word?

ORGON I don't say that.

CLEANTE I hope no obstacle Can keep you from performing what you've promised.

ORGON Well, that depends.

CLEANTE Why must you beat about? Valere has sent me here to settle matters.

ORGON Heaven be praised!

CLEANTE What answer shall I take him?

ORGON Why, anything you please.

CLEANTE But we must know Your plans. What are they?

ORGON I shall do the will Of Heaven.

CLEANTE Come, be serious. You've given Your promise to Valere. Now will you keep it?

ORGON Good-bye.

CLEANTE (alone) His love, methinks, has much to fear; I must go let him know what's happening here.

Act 2

Scene 1

ORGON, MARIANE

ORGON Now, Mariane.

MARIANE Yes, father?

ORGON Come; I'll tell you A secret.

MARIANE Yes ... What are you looking for?

ORGON (looking into a small closet-room) To see there's no one there to spy upon us; That little closet's mighty fit to hide in. There! We're all right now. Mariane, in you I've always found a daughter dutiful And gentle. So I've always love you dearly.

MARIANE I'm grateful for your fatherly affection.

ORGON Well spoken, daughter. Now, prove you deserve it By doing as I wish in all respects.

MARIANE To do so is the height of my ambition.

ORGON Excellent well. What say you of—Tartuffe?

MARIANE Who? I?

ORGON Yes, you. Look to it how you answer.

MARIANE Why! I'll say of him—anything you please.

Scene 2

ORGON, MARIANE, DORINE (coming in quietly and standing behind Orgon, so that he does not see her)

ORGON Well spoken. A good girl. Say then, my daughter, That all his person shines with noble merit, That he has won your heart, and you would like To have him, by my choice, become your husband. Eh?

MARIANE Eh?

ORGON What say you?

MARIANE Please, what did you say?

ORGON What?

MARIANE Surely I mistook you, sir?

ORGON How now?

MARIANE Who is it, father, you would have me say Has won my heart, and I would like to have Become my husband, by your choice?

ORGON Tartuffe.

MARIANE But, father, I protest it isn't true! Why should you make me tell this dreadful lie?

ORGON Because I mean to have it be the truth. Let this suffice for you: I've settled it.

MARIANE What, father, you would ... ?

ORGON Yes, child, I'm resolved To graft Tartuffe into my family. So he must be your husband. That I've settled. And since your duty ..

(Seeing Dorine) What are you doing there? Your curiosity is keen, my girl, To make you come eavesdropping on us so.

DORINE Upon my word, I don't know how the rumour Got started—if 'twas guess-work or mere chance But I had heard already of this match, And treated it as utter stuff and nonsense.

ORGON What! Is the thing incredible?

DORINE So much so I don't believe it even from yourself, sir.

ORGON I know a way to make you credit it.

DORINE No, no, you're telling us a fairly tale!

ORGON I'm telling you just what will happen shortly.

DORINE Stuff!

ORGON Daughter, what I say is in good earnest.

DORINE There, there, don't take your father seriously; He's fooling.

ORGON But I tell you ...

DORINE No. No use. They won't believe you.

ORGON If I let my anger ...

DORINE Well, then, we do believe you; and the worse For you it is. What! Can a grown-up man With that expanse of beard across his face Be mad enough to want ...?

ORGON You hark me: You've taken on yourself here in this house A sort of free familiarity That I don't like, I tell you frankly, girl.

DORINE There, there, let's not get angry, sir, I beg you. But are you making game of everybody? Your daughter's not cut out for bigot's meat; And he has more important things to think of. Besides, what can you gain by such a match? How can a man of wealth, like you, go choose A wretched vagabond for son-in-law?

ORGON You hold your tongue. And know, the less he has, The better cause have we to honour him. His poverty is honest poverty; It should exalt him more than worldly grandeur, For he has let himself be robbed of all, Through careless disregard of temporal things And fixed attachment to the things eternal. My help may set him on his feet again, Win back his property—a fair estate He has at home, so I'm informed—and prove him For what he is, a true-born gentleman.

(Pie·us)

DORINE Yes, so he says himself. Such vanity But ill accords with pious living, sir. The man who cares for holiness alone Should not so loudly boast his name and birth; The humble ways of genuine <u>devoutness</u> Brook not so much display of earthly pride. Why should he be so vain? ... But I offend you: Let's leave his rank, then,—take the man himself: Can you without compunction give a (Guilt) man Like him possession of a girl like her? Think what a scandal's sure to come of it! Virtue is at the mercy of the fates, When a girl's married to a man she hates; The best intent to live an honest woman Depends upon the husband's being human, And men whose brows are pointed at afar May thank themselves their wives are what they are. For to be true is more than woman can, With husbands built upon a certain plan; And he who weds his child against her will Owes heaven account for it, if she do ill. Think then what perils wait on your design.

(Apparel)·Danger

ORGON (to Mariane) So! I must learn what's what from her, you see!

DORINE You might do worse than follow my advice.

ORGON Daughter, we can't waste time upon this nonsense; I know what's good for you, and I'm your father. True, I had promised you to young Valere; But, first, they tell me he's inclined to gamble, And then, I fear his faith is not quite sound. I haven't noticed that he's regular At church.

DORINE You'd have him run there just when you do. Like those who go on purpose to be seen?

27

ORGON I don't ask your opinion on the matter. In short, the other is in Heaven's best graces, And that is riches quite beyond compare. This match will bring you every joy you long for; 'Twill be all steeped in sweetness and delight. You'll live together, in your faithful loves, Like two sweet children, like two turtle-doves; You'll never fail to quarrel, scold, or tease, And you may do with him whate'er you please.

DORINE With him? Do naught but give him horns, I'll warrant.

ORGON Out on thee, wench!

DORINE I tell you he's cut out for't; However great your daughter's virtue, sir, His destiny is sure to prove the stronger.

ORGON Have done with interrupting. Hold your tongue. Don't poke your nose in other people's business.

DORINE (She keeps interrupting him, just as he turns and starts to speak to his daughter). If I make bold, sir, 'tis for your own good.

ORGON You're too officious; pray you, hold your tongue.

DORINE 'Tis love of you ...

ORGON I want none of your love.

DORINE Then I will love you in your own despite.

ORGON You will, eh?

DORINE Yes, your honour's dear to me; I can't endure to see you made the butt Of all men's ridicule.

ORGON Won't you be still?

DORINE 'Twould be a sin to let you make this match.

ORGON Won't you be still, I say, you impudent viper!

DORINE What! you are pious, and you lose your temper?

ORGON I'm all wrought up, with your confounded nonsense; Now, once for all, I tell you hold your tongue.

DORINE Then mum's the word; I'll take it out in thinking.

ORGON Think all you please; but not a syllable To me about it, or ... you understand!

(Turning to his daughter.) As a wise father, I've considered all With due deliberation.

DORINE I'll go mad If I can't speak. (She stops the instant he turns his head.)

ORGON Though he's no lady's man, Tartuffe is well enough ...

DORINE A pretty phiz!

ORGON So that, although you may not care at all For his best qualities ...

DORINE A handsome dowry!

(Orgon turns and stands in front of her, with arms folded, eyeing her.) Were I in her place, any man should rue it Who married me by force, that's mighty certain; I'd let him know, and that within a week, A woman's vengeance isn't far to seek.

ORGON (to Dorine) So—nothing that I say has any weight?

DORINE Eh? What's wrong now? I didn't speak to you.

ORGON What were you doing?

DORINE Talking to myself.

ORGON Oh! Very well. (Aside.) Her monstrous impudence Must be chastised with one good slap in the face.

29

(He stands ready to strike her, and, each time he speaks to his daughter, he glances toward her; but she stands still and says not a word.)

ORGON Daughter, you must approve of my design.... Think of this husband ... I have chosen for you...

(To Dorine) Why don't you talk to yourself?

DORINE Nothing to say.

ORGON One little word more.

DORINE Oh, no, thanks. Not now.

ORGON Sure, I'd have caught you.

DORINE Faith, I'm no such fool.

ORGON So, daughter, now obedience is the word; You must accept my choice with reverence.

DORINE (running away) You'd never catch me marrying such a creature.

ORGON (swinging his hand at her and missing her) Daughter, you've such a pestilent hussy there I can't live with her longer, without sin. I can't discuss things in the state I'm in. My mind's so flustered by her insolent talk, To calm myself, I must go take a walk.

Scene 3

MARIANE, DORINE

DORINE Say, have you lost the tongue from out your head? And must I speak your role from A to Zed? You let them broach a project that's absurd, And don't oppose it with a single word!

MARIANE What can I do? My father is the master.

DORINE Do? Everything, to ward off such disaster.

MARIANE But what?

DORINE Tell him one doesn't love by proxy; Tell him you'll marry for yourself, not him; Since you're the one for whom the thing is done, You are the one, not he, the man must please; If his Tartuffe has charmed him so, why let him Just marry him himself—no one will hinder.

MARIANE A father's rights are such, it seems to me, That I could never dare to say a word.

DORINE Came, talk it out. Valere has asked your hand: Now do you love him, pray, or do you not?

MARIANE Dorine! How can you wrong my love so much, And ask me such a question? Have I not A hundred times laid bare my heart to you? Do you know how ardently I love him?

DORINE How do I know if heart and words agree, And if in honest truth you really love him?

MARIANE Dorine, you wrong me greatly if you doubt it; I've shown my inmost feelings, all too plainly.

DORINE So then, you love him?

MARIANE Yes, devotedly.

DORINE And he returns your love, apparently?

MARIANE I think so.

DORINE And you both alike are eager To be well married to each other?

MARIANE Surely.

DORINE Then what's your plan about this other match?

MARIANE To kill myself, if it is forced upon me.

DORINE Good! That's a remedy I hadn't thought of. Just die, and everything will be all right. This medicine is marvellous, indeed! It drives me mad to hear folk talk such nonsense.

MARIANE Oh dear, Dorine you get in such a temper! You have no sympathy for people's troubles.

DORINE I have no sympathy when folk talk nonsense, And flatten out as you do, at a pinch.

MARIANE But what can you expect?—if one is timid?—

DORINE But what is love worth, if it has no courage?

MARIANE Am I not constant in my love for him? Is't not his place to win me from my father?

DORINE But if your father is a crazy fool, And quite bewitched with his Tartuffe? And breaks His bounden word? Is that your lover's fault?

MARIANE But shall I publicly refuse and scorn This match, and make it plain that I'm in love? Shall I cast off for him, whate'er he be, Womanly modesty and filial duty? You ask me to display my love in public ... ?

32

DORINE No, no, I ask you nothing. You shall be Mister Tartuffe's; why, now I think of it, I should be wrong to turn you from this marriage. What cause can I have to oppose your wishes? So fine a match! An excellent good match! Mister Tartuffe! Oh ho! No mean proposal! Mister Tartuffe, sure, take it all in all, Is not a man to sneeze at—oh, by no means! 'Tis no small luck to be his happy spouse. The whole world joins to sing his praise already; He's noble—in his parish; handsome too; Red ears and high complexion—oh, my lud! You'll be too happy, sure, with him for husband.

MARIANE Oh dear! ...

DORINE What joy and pride will fill your heart To be the bride of such a handsome fellow!

MARIANE Oh, stop, I beg you; try to find some way To help break off the match. I quite give in, I'm ready to do anything you say.

DORINE No, no, a daughter must obey her father, Though he should want to make her wed a monkey. Besides, your fate is fine. What could be better! You'll take the stage-coach to his little village, And find it full of uncles and of cousins, Whose conversation will delight you. Then You'll be presented in their best society. You'll even go to call, by way of welcome, On Mrs. Bailiff, Mrs. Tax-Collector, Who'll patronise you with a folding-stool. There, once a year, at carnival, you'll have Perhaps—a ball; with orchestra—two bag-pipes; And sometimes a trained ape, and Punch and Judy; Though if your husband ...

MARIANE Oh, you'll kill me. Please Contrive to help me out with your advice.

DORINE I thank you kindly.

MARIANE Oh! Dorine, I beg you ...

DORINE To serve you right, this marriage must go through.

MARIANE Dear girl!

DORINE No.

33

MARIANE If I say I love Valere ...

DORINE No, no. Tartuffe's your man, and you shall taste him.

MARIANE You know I've always trusted you; now help me ...

DORINE No, you shall be, my faith! Tartuffified.

MARIANE Well, then, since you've no pity for my fate Let me take counsel only of despair; It will advise and help and give me courage; There's one sure cure, I know, for all my troubles.

(She starts to go.)

DORINE There, there! Come back. I can't be angry long. I must take pity on you, after all.

MARIANE Oh, don't you see, Dorine, if I must bear This martyrdom, I certainly shall die.

DORINE Now don't you fret. We'll surely find some way. To hinder this ... But here's Valere, your lover.

Scene 4

VALERE, MARIANE, DORINE

VALERE Madam, a piece of news—quite new to me— Has just come out, and very fine it is.

MARIANE What piece of news?

VALERE Your marriage with Tartuffe.

MARIANE 'Tis true my father has this plan in mind.

VALERE Your father, madam ...

MARIANE Yes, he's changed his plans, And did but now propose it to me.

VALERE What! Seriously?

MARIANE Yes, he was serious, And openly insisted on the match.

VALERE And what's your resolution in the matter, Madam?

MARIANE I don't know.

VALERE That's a pretty answer. You don't know?

MARIANE No.

VALERE No?

MARIANE What do you advise?

VALERE I? My advice is, marry him, by all means.

MARIANE That's your advice?

VALERE Yes.

MARIANE Do you mean it?

VALERE Surely. A splendid choice, and worthy of your acceptance.

MARIANE Oh, very well, sir! I shall take your counsel.

VALERE You'll find no trouble taking it, I warrant.

MARIANE No more than you did giving it, be sure.

VALERE I gave it, truly, to oblige you, madam.

MARIANE And I shall take it to oblige you, sir.

Dorine (withdrawing to the back of the stage) Let's see what this affair will come to.

VALERE So, That is your love? And it was all deceit When you ...

MARIANE I beg you, say no more of that. You told me, squarely, sir, I should accept The husband that is offered me; and I Will tell you squarely that I mean to do so, Since you have given me this good advice.

VALERE Don't shield yourself with talk of my advice. You had your mind made up, that's evident; And now you're snatching at a trifling pretext To justify the breaking of your word.

MARIANE Exactly so.

VALERE Of course it is; your heart Has never known true love for me.

MARIANE Alas! You're free to think so, if you please.

VALERE Yes, yes, I'm free to think so; and my outraged love May yet forestall you in your perfidy, And offer elsewhere both my heart and hand.

MARIANE No doubt of it; the love your high deserts May win ...

VALERE Good Lord, have done with my deserts! I know I have but few, and you have proved it. But I may find more kindness in another; I know of someone, who'll not be ashamed To take your leavings, and make up my loss.

MARIANE The loss is not so great; you'll easily Console yourself completely for this change.

VALERE I'll try my best, that you may well believe. When we're forgotten by a woman's heart, Our pride is challenged; we, too, must forget; Or if we cannot, must at least pretend to. No other way can man such baseness prove, As be a lover scorned, and still in love.

MARIANE In faith, a high and noble sentiment.

VALERE Yes; and it's one that all men must approve. What! Would you have me keep my love alive, And see you fly into another's arms Before my very eyes; and never offer To someone else the heart that you had scorned?

MARIANE Oh, no, indeed! For my part, I could wish That it were done already.

VALERE What! You wish it?

MARIANE Yes.

VALERE This is insult heaped on injury; I'll go at once and do as you desire.

(He takes a step or two as if to go away.)

MARIANE Oh, very well then.

VALERE (turning back) But remember this. 'Twas you that drove me to this desperate pass.

MARIANE Of course.

VALERE (turning back again) And in the plan that I have formed I only follow your example.

MARIANE Yes.

VALERE (at the door) Enough; you shall be punctually obeyed.

MARIANE So much the better.

VALERE (coming back again) This is once for all.

MARIANE So be it, then.

VALERE (He goes toward the door, but just as he reaches it, turns around) Eh?

MARIANE What?

VALERE You didn't call me?

MARIANE I? You are dreaming.

VALERE Very well, I'm gone. Madam, farewell.

(He walks slowly away.)

MARIANE Farewell, sir.

DORINE I must say You've lost your senses and both gone clean daft! I've let you fight it out to the end o' the chapter To see how far the thing could go. Oho, there, Mister Valere!

(She goes and seizes him by the arm, to stop him. He makes a great show of resistance.)

VALERE What do you want, Dorine?

DORINE Come here.

VALERE No, no, I'm quite beside myself. Don't hinder me from doing as she wishes.

DORINE Stop!

VALERE No. You see, I'm fixed, resolved, determined.

DORINE So!

MARIANE (aside) Since my presence pains him, makes him go, I'd better go myself, and leave him free.

DORINE (leaving Valere, and running after Mariane) Now t'other! Where are you going?

MARIANE Let me be.

DORINE. Come back.

MARIANE No, no, it isn't any use.

VALERE (aside) 'Tis clear the sight of me is torture to her; No doubt, t'were better I should free her from it.

DORINE (leaving Mariane and running after Valere) Same thing again! Deuce take you both, I say. Now stop your fooling; come here, you; and you.

(She pulls first one, then the other, toward the middle of the stage.)

VALERE (to Dorine) What's your idea?

MARIANE (to Dorine) What can you mean to do?

DORINE Set you to rights, and pull you out o' the scrape.

(To Valere) Are you quite mad, to quarrel with her now?

VALERE Didn't you hear the things she said to me?

DORINE (to Mariane) Are you quite mad, to get in such a passion?

MARIANE Didn't you see the way he treated me?

DORINE Fools, both of you.

(To Valere) She thinks of nothing else But to keep faith with you, I vouch for it.

(To Mariane) And he loves none but you, and longs for nothing But just to marry you, I stake my life on't.

MARIANE (to Valere) Why did you give me such advice then, pray?

VALERE (to Mariane) Why ask for my advice on such a matter?

DORINE You both are daft, I tell you. Here, your hands.

(To Valere) Come, yours.

VALERE (giving Dorine his hand) What for?

DORINE (to Mariane) Now, yours.

MARIANE (giving Dorine her hand) But what's the use?

DORINE Oh, quick now, come along. There, both of you— You love each other better than you think.

(Valere and Mariane hold each other's hands some time without looking at each other.)

VALERE (at last turning toward Mariane) Come, don't be so ungracious now about it; Look at a man as if you didn't hate him.

(Mariane looks sideways toward Valere, with just a bit of a smile.)

DORINE My faith and troth, what fools these lovers be!

VALERE (to Mariane) But come now, have I not a just complaint? And truly, are you not a wicked creature To take delight in saying what would pain me?

MARIANE And are you not yourself the most ungrateful ... ?

DORINE Leave this discussion till another time; Now, think how you'll stave off this plaguy marriage.

MARIANE Then tell us how to go about it.

DORINE Well, We'll try all sorts of ways.

(To Mariane) Your father's daft;

(To Valere) This plan is nonsense.

(To Mariane) You had better humour His notions by a semblance of consent, So that in case of danger, you can still Find means to block the marriage by delay. If you gain time, the rest is easy, trust me. One day you'll fool them with a sudden illness, Causing delay; another day, ill omens: You've met a funeral, or broke a mirror, Or dreamed of muddy water. Best of all, They cannot marry you to anyone Without your saying yes. But now, methinks, They mustn't find you chattering together.

(To Valere) You, go at once and set your friends at work To make him keep his word to you; while we Will bring the brother's influence to bear, And get the step-mother on our side, too. Good-bye.

VALERE (to Mariane) Whatever efforts we may make, My greatest hope, be sure, must rest on you.

MARIANE (to Valere) I cannot answer for my father's whims; But no one save Valere shall ever have me.

VALERE You thrill me through with joy! Whatever comes ...

DORINE Oho! These lovers! Never done with prattling! Now go.

VALERE (starting to go, and coming back again) One last word ...

DORINE What a gabble and pother! Be off! By this door, you. And you, by t'other.

(She pushes them off, by the shoulders, in opposite directions.)

Act 3

Scene 1

DAMIS, DORINE

DAMIS May lightning strike me dead this very instant, May I be everywhere proclaimed a scoundrel, If any reverence or power shall stop me, And if I don't do straightway something desperate!

DORINE I beg you, moderate this towering passion; Your father did but merely mention it. Not all things that are talked of turn to facts; The road is long, sometimes, from plans to acts.

DAMIS No, I must end this paltry fellow's plots, And he shall hear from me a truth or two.

DORINE So ho! Go slow now. Just you leave the fellow— Your father too— in your step-mother's hands. She has some influence with this Tartuffe, He makes a point of heeding all she says, And I suspect that he is fond of her. Would God 'twere true!—'Twould be the height of humour Now, she has sent for him, in your behalf, To sound him on this marriage, to find out What his ideas are, and to show him plainly What troubles he may cause, if he persists In giving countenance to this design. His man says, he's at prayers, I mustn't see him, But likewise says, he'll presently be down. So off with you, and let me wait for him.

DAMIS I may be present at this interview.

DORINE No, no! They must be left alone.

DAMIS I won't So much as speak to him.

DORINE Go on! We know you And your high tantrums. Just the way to spoil things! Be off.

DAMIS No, I must see—I'll keep my temper.

DORINE Out on you, what a plague! He's coming. Hide!

(Damis goes and hides in the closet at the back of the stage.)

Scene 2

TARTUFFE, DORINE

TARTUFFE (speaking to his valet, off the stage, as soon as he sees Dorine is there) Lawrence, put up my hair-cloth shirt and scourge, And pray that Heaven may shed its light upon you. If any come to see me, say I'm gone To share my alms among the prisoners.

DORINE (aside) What affectation and what showing off!

TARTUFFE What do you want with me?

DORINE To tell you ...

TARTUFFE (taking a handkerchief from his pocket) Ah! Before you speak, pray take this handkerchief.

DORINE What?

TARTUFFE Cover up that bosom, which I can't Endure to look on. Things like that offend Our souls, and fill our minds with sinful thoughts.

DORINE Are you so tender to temptation, then, And has the flesh such power upon your senses? I don't know how you get in such a heat; For my part, I am not so prone to lust, And I could see you stripped from head to foot, And all your hide not tempt me in the least.

TARTUFFE Show in your speech some little modesty, Or I must instantly take leave of you.

DORINE No, no, I'll leave you to yourself; I've only One thing to say: Madam will soon be down, And begs the favour of a word with you.

TARTUFFE Ah! Willingly.

46

DORINE (aside) How gentle all at once! My faith, I still believe I've hit upon it.

TARTUFFE Will she come soon?

DORINE I think I hear her now. Yes, here she is herself; I'll leave you with her.

Scene 3

ELMIRE, TARTUFFE

TARTUFFE May Heaven's overflowing kindness ever Give you good health of body and of soul, And bless your days according to the wishes And prayers of its most humble votary!

ELMIRE I'm very grateful for your pious wishes. But let's sit down, so we may talk at ease.

TARTUFFE (after sitting down) And how are you recovered from your illness?

ELMIRE (sitting down also) Quite well; the fever soon let go its hold.

TARTUFFE My prayers, I fear, have not sufficient merit To have drawn down this favour from on high; But each entreaty that I made to Heaven Had for its object your recovery.

ELMIRE You're too solicitous on my behalf.

TARTUFFE We could not cherish your dear health too much; I would have given mine, to help restore it.

ELMIRE That's pushing Christian charity too far; I owe you many thanks for so much kindness.

TARTUFFE I do far less for you than you deserve.

ELMIRE There is a matter that I wished to speak of In private; I am glad there's no one here To listen.

TARTUFFE Madam, I am overjoyed. 'Tis sweet to find myself alone with you. This is an opportunity I've asked Of Heaven, many a time; till now, in vain.

ELMIRE All that I wish, is just a word from you, Quite frank and open, hiding nothing from me.

(DAMIS, without their seeing him, opens the closet door halfway.)

TARTUFFE I too could wish, as Heaven's especial favour, To lay my soul quite open to your eyes, And swear to you, the trouble that I made About those visits which your charms attract, Does not result from any hatred toward you, But rather from a passionate devotion, And purest motives ...

ELMIRE That is how I take it, I think 'tis my salvation that concerns you.

TARTUFFE (pressing her finger tips) Madam, 'tis so; and such is my devotion ...

ELMIRE Ouch! but you squeeze too hard.

TARTUFFE Excess of zeal. In no way could I ever mean to hurt you, And I'd as soon ...

(He puts his hand on her knee.)

ELMIRE What's your hand doing there?

TARTUFFE Feeling your gown; the stuff is very soft.

ELMIRE Let be, I beg you; I am very ticklish.

(She moves her chair away, and Tartuffe brings his nearer.)

TARTUFFE (handling the lace yoke of Elmire's dress) Dear me how wonderful in workmanship This lace is! They do marvels, nowadays; Things of all kinds were never better made.

ELMIRE Yes, very true. But let us come to business. They say my husband means to break his word. And marry Mariane to you. Is't so?

TARTUFFE He did hint some such thing; but truly, madam, That's not the happiness I'm yearning after; I see elsewhere the sweet compelling charms Of such a joy as fills my every wish.

ELMIRE You mean you cannot love terrestrial things.

TARTUFFE The heart within my bosom is not stone.

ELMIRE I well believe your sighs all tend to Heaven, And nothing here below can stay your thoughts.

TARTUFFE Love for the beauty of eternal things Cannot destroy our love for earthly beauty; Our mortal senses well may be entranced By perfect works that Heaven has fashioned here. Its charms reflected shine in such as you, And in yourself, its rarest miracles; It has displayed such marvels in your face, That eyes are dazed, and hearts are rapt away; I could not look on you, the perfect creature, Without admiring Nature's great Creator, And feeling all my heart inflamed with love For you, His fairest image of Himself. At first I trembled lest this secret love Might be the Evil Spirit's artful snare; I even schooled my heart to flee your beauty, Thinking it was a bar to my salvation. But soon, enlightened, O all lovely one, I saw how this my passion may be blameless, How I may make it fit with modesty, And thus completely yield my heart to it. 'Tis I must own, a great presumption in me To dare make you the offer of my heart; My love hopes all things from your perfect goodness, And nothing from my own poor weak endeavour. You are my hope, my stay, my peace of heart; On you depends my torment or my bliss; And by your doom of judgment, I shall be Blest, if you will; or damned, by your decree.

ELMIRE Your declaration's turned most gallantly; But truly, it is just a bit surprising. You should have better armed your heart, methinks, And taken thought somewhat on such a matter. A pious man like you, known everywhere ...

TARTUFFE Though pious, I am none the less a man; And when a man beholds your heavenly charms, The heart surrenders, and can think no more. I know such words seem strange, coming from me; But, madam, I'm no angel, after all; If you condemn my frankly made avowal You only have your charming self to blame. Soon as I saw your more than human beauty, You were thenceforth the sovereign of my soul; Sweetness ineffable was in your eyes, That took by storm my still resisting heart, And conquered everything, fasts, prayers, and tears,

And turned my worship wholly to yourself. My looks, my sighs, have spoke a thousand times; Now, to express it all, my voice must speak. If but you will look down with gracious favour Upon the sorrows of your worthless slave, If in your goodness you will give me comfort And condescend unto my nothingness, I'll ever pay you, O sweet miracle, An unexampled worship and devotion. Then too, with me your honour runs no risk; With me you need not fear a public scandal. These court gallants, that women are so fond of, Are boastful of their acts, and vain in speech; They always brag in public of their progress; Soon as a favour's granted, they'll divulge it; Their tattling tongues, if you but trust to them, Will foul the altar where their hearts have worshipped. But men like me are so discreet in love, That you may trust their lasting secrecy. The care we take to guard our own good name May fully guarantee the one we love; So you may find, with hearts like ours sincere, Love without scandal, pleasure without fear.

ELMIRE I've heard you through—your speech is clear, at least. But don't you fear that I may take a fancy To tell my husband of your gallant passion, And that a prompt report of this affair May somewhat change the friendship which he bears you?

TARTUFFE I know that you're too good and generous, That you will pardon my temerity, Excuse, upon the score of human frailty, The violence of passion that offends you, And not forget, when you consult your mirror, That I'm not blind, and man is made of flesh.

ELMIRE Some women might do otherwise, perhaps, But I am willing to employ discretion, And not repeat the matter to my husband; But in return, I'll ask one thing of you: That you urge forward, frankly and sincerely, The marriage of Valere to Mariane; That you give up the unjust influence By which you hope to win another's rights; And ...

Scene 4

ELMIRE, DAMIS, TARTUFFE

DAMIS (coming out of the closet-room where he had been hiding) No, I say! This thing must be made public. I was just there, and overheard it all; And Heaven's goodness must have brought me there On purpose to confound this scoundrel's pride And grant me means to take a signal vengeance On his hypocrisy and arrogance, And undeceive my father, showing up The rascal caught at making love to you.

ELMIRE No, no; it is enough if he reforms, Endeavouring to deserve the favour shown him. And since I've promised, do not you belie me. 'Tis not my way to make a public scandal; An honest wife will scorn to heed such follies, And never fret her husband's ears with them.

DAMIS You've reasons of your own for acting thus; And I have mine for doing otherwise. To spare him now would be a mockery; His bigot's pride has triumphed all too long Over my righteous anger, and has caused Far too much trouble in our family. The rascal all too long has ruled my father, And crossed my sister's love, and mine as well. The traitor now must be unmasked before him: And Providence has given me means to do it. To Heaven I owe the opportunity, And if I did not use it now I have it, I should deserve to lose it once for all.

ELMIRE Damis ...

DAMIS No, by your leave; I'll not be counselled. I'm overjoyed. You needn't try to tell me I must give up the pleasure of revenge. I'll make an end of this affair at once; And, to content me, here's my father now.

Scene 5

ORGON, ELMIRE, DAMIS, TARTUFFE

DAMIS Father, we've news to welcome your arrival, That's altogether novel, and surprising. You are well paid for your caressing care, And this fine gentleman rewards your love Most handsomely, with zeal that seeks no less Than your dishonour, as has now been proven. I've just surprised him making to your wife The shameful offer of a guilty love. She, somewhat over gentle and discreet, Insisted that the thing should be concealed; But I will not condone such shamelessness, Nor so far wrong you as to keep it secret.

ELMIRE Yes, I believe a wife should never trouble Her husband's peace of mind with such vain gossip; A woman's honour does not hang on telling; It is enough if she defend herself; Or so I think; Damis, you'd not have spoken, If you would but have heeded my advice.

Scene 6

ORGON, DAMIS, TARTUFFE

ORGON Just Heaven! Can what I hear be credited?

TARTUFFE Yes, brother, I am wicked, I am guilty, A miserable sinner, steeped in evil, The greatest criminal that ever lived. Each moment of my life is stained with soilures; And all is but a mass of crime and filth; Heaven, for my punishment, I see it plainly, Would mortify me now. Whatever wrong They find to charge me with, I'll not deny it But guard against the pride of self-defence. Believe their stories, arm your wrath against me, And drive me like a villain from your house; I cannot have so great a share of shame But what I have deserved a greater still.

ORGON (to his son) You miscreant, can you dare, with such a falsehood, To try to stain the whiteness of his virtue?

DAMIS What! The feigned meekness of this hypocrite Makes you discredit

ORGON Silence, cursed plague!

TARTUFFE Ah! Let him speak; you chide him wrongfully; You'd do far better to believe his tales. Why favour me so much in such a matter? How can you know of what I'm capable? And should you trust my outward semblance, brother, Or judge therefrom that I'm the better man? No, no; you let appearances deceive you; I'm anything but what I'm thought to be, Alas! and though all men believe me godly, The simple truth is, I'm a worthless creature.

(To Damis) Yes, my dear son, say on, and call me traitor, Abandoned scoundrel, thief, and murderer; Heap on me names yet more detestable, And I shall not gainsay you; I've deserved them; I'll bear this ignominy on my knees, To expiate in shame the crimes I've done.

ORGON (to Tartuffe) Ah, brother, 'tis too much!

54

(To his son) You'll not relent, You blackguard?

DAMIS What! His talk can so deceive you ...

ORGON Silence, you scoundrel!

(To Tartuffe) Brother, rise, I beg you.

(To his son) Infamous villain!

DAMIS Can he ...

ORGON Silence!

DAMIS What ...

ORGON Another word, I'll break your every bone.

TARTUFFE Brother, in God's name, don't be angry with him! I'd rather bear myself the bitterest torture Than have him get a scratch on my account.

ORGON (to his son) Ungrateful monster!

TARTUFFE Stop. Upon my knees I beg you pardon him ...

ORGON (throwing himself on his knees too, and embracing Tartuffe) Alas! How can you?

(To his son) Villain! Behold his goodness!

DAMIS So ...

ORGON Be still.

DAMIS What! I ...

ORGON Be still, I say. I know your motives For this attack. You hate him, all of you; Wife, children, servants, all let loose upon him, You have recourse to every shameful trick To drive this godly man out of my house; The more you

55

strive to rid yourselves of him, The more I'll strive to make him stay with me; I'll have him straightway married to my daughter, Just to confound the pride of all of you.

DAMIS What! Will you force her to accept his hand?

ORGON Yes, and this very evening, to enrage you, Young rascal! Ah! I'll brave you all, and show you That I'm the master, and must be obeyed. Now, down upon your knees this instant, rogue, And take back what you said, and ask his pardon.

DAMIS Who? I? Ask pardon of that cheating scoundrel ... ?

ORGON Do you resist, you beggar, and insult him? A cudgel, here! a cudgel!

(To Tartuffe) Don't restrain me.

(To his son) Off with you! Leave my house this instant, sirrah, And never dare set foot in it again.

DAMIS Yes, I will leave your house, but ...

ORGON Leave it quickly. You reprobate, I disinherit you, And give you, too, my curse into the bargain.

*

Scene 7

ORGON, TARTUFFE

ORGON What! So insult a saintly man of God!

TARTUFFE Heaven, forgive him all the pain he gives me! [4]

[Footnote 4: Some modern editions have adopted the reading, preserved by tradition as that of the earliest stage version: Heaven, forgive him even as I forgive him! Voltaire gives still another reading: Heaven, forgive me even as I forgive him! Whichever was the original version, it appears in none of the early editions, and Moliere probably felt forced to change it on account of its too close resemblance to the Biblical phrase.]

(To Orgon) Could you but know with what distress I see Them try to vilify me to my brother!

ORGON Ah!

TARTUFFE The mere thought of such ingratitude Makes my soul suffer torture, bitterly ... My horror at it ... Ah! my heart's so full I cannot speak ... I think I'll die of it.

ORGON (in tears, running to the door through which he drove away his son) Scoundrel! I wish I'd never let you go, But slain you on the spot with my own hand.

(To Tartuffe) Brother, compose yourself, and don't be angry.

TARTUFFE Nay, brother, let us end these painful quarrels. I see what troublous times I bring upon you, And think 'tis needful that I leave this house.

ORGON What! You can't mean it?

TARTUFFE Yes, they hate me here, And try, I find, to make you doubt my faith.

ORGON What of it? Do you find I listen to them?

TARTUFFE No doubt they won't stop there. These same reports You now reject, may some day win a hearing.

ORGON No, brother, never.

TARTUFFE Ah! my friend, a woman May easily mislead her husband's mind.

ORGON No, no.

TARTUFFE So let me quickly go away And thus remove all cause for such attacks.

ORGON No, you shall stay; my life depends upon it.

TARTUFFE Then I must mortify myself. And yet, If you should wish ...

ORGON No, never!

TARTUFFE Very well, then; No more of that. But I shall rule my conduct To fit the case. Honour is delicate, And friendship binds me to forestall suspicion, Prevent all scandal, and avoid your wife.

ORGON No, you shall haunt her, just to spite them all. 'Tis my delight to set them in a rage; You shall be seen together at all hours And what is more, the better to defy them, I'll have no other heir but you; and straightway I'll go and make a deed of gift to you, Drawn in due form, of all my property. A good true friend, my son-in-law to be, Is more to me than son, and wife, and kindred. You will accept my offer, will you not?

TARTUFFE Heaven's will be done in everything!

ORGON Poor man! We'll go make haste to draw the deed aright, And then let envy burst itself with spite!

Act 4

Scene 1

CLEANTE, TARTUFFE

CLEANTE Yes, it's become the talk of all the town, And make a stir that's scarcely to your credit; And I have met you, sir, most opportunely, To tell you in a word my frank opinion. Not to sift out this scandal to the bottom, Suppose the worst for us—suppose Damis Acted the traitor, and accused you falsely; Should not a Christian pardon this offence, And stifle in his heart all wish for vengeance? Should you permit that, for your petty quarrel, A son be driven from his father's house? I tell you yet again, and tell you frankly, Everyone, high or low, is scandalised; If you'll take my advice, you'll make it up, And not push matters to extremities. Make sacrifice to God of your resentment; Restore the son to favour with his father.

TARTUFFE Alas! So far as I'm concerned, how gladly Would I do so! I bear him no ill will; I pardon all, lay nothing to his charge, And wish with all my heart that I might serve him; But Heaven's interests cannot allow it; If he returns, then I must leave the house. After his conduct, quite unparalleled, All intercourse between us would bring scandal; God knows what everyone's first thought would be! They would attribute it to merest scheming On my part—say that conscious of my guilt I feigned a Christian love for my accuser, But feared him in my heart, and hoped to win him And underhandedly secure his silence.

CLEANTE You try to put us off with specious phrases; But all your arguments are too far-fetched. Why take upon yourself the cause of Heaven? Does Heaven need our help to punish sinners? Leave to itself the care of its own vengeance, And keep in mind the pardon it commands us; Besides, think somewhat less of men's opinions, When you are following the will of Heaven. Shall petty fear of what the world may think Prevent the doing of a noble deed? No!—let us always do as Heaven commands, And not perplex our brains with further questions.

TARTUFFE Already I have told you I forgive him; And that is doing, sir, as Heaven commands. But after this day's scandal and affront Heaven does not order me to live with him.

CLEANTE And does it order you to lend your ear To what mere whim suggested to his father, And to accept gift of his estates, On which, in justice, you can make no claim?

TARTUFFE No one who knows me, sir, can have the thought That I am acting from a selfish motive. The goods of this world have no charms for me; I am not dazzled by their treacherous glamour; And if I bring myself to take the gift Which he insists on giving me, I do so, To tell the truth, only because I fear This whole estate may fall into bad hands, And those to whom it comes may use it ill And not employ it, as is my design, For Heaven's glory and my neighbours' good.

CLEANTE Eh, sir, give up these conscientious scruples That well may cause a rightful heir's complaints. Don't take so much upon yourself, but let him Possess what's his, at his own risk and peril; Consider, it were better he misused it, Than you should be accused of robbing him. I am astounded that unblushingly You could allow such offers to be made! Tell me—has true religion any maxim That teaches us to rob the lawful heir? If Heaven has made it quite impossible Damis and you should live together here, Were it not better you should quietly And honourably withdraw, than let the son Be driven out for your sake, dead against All reason? 'Twould be giving, sir, believe me, Such an example of your probity ...

TARTUFFE Sir, it is half-past three; certain devotions Recall me to my closet; you'll forgive me For leaving you so soon.

CLEANTE (alone) Ah!

Scene 2

ELMIRE, MARIANE, CLEANTE, DORINE

DORINE (to Cleante) Sir, we beg you To help us all you can in her behalf; She's suffering almost more than heart can bear; This match her father means to make to-night Drives her each moment to despair. He's coming. Let us unite our efforts now, we beg you, And try by strength or skill to change his purpose.

Scene 3

ORGON, ELMIRE, MARIANE, CLEANTE, DORINE

ORGON So ho! I'm glad to find you all together.

(To Mariane) Here is the contract that shall make you happy, My dear. You know already what it means.

MARIANE (on her knees before Orgon) Father, I beg you, in the name of Heaven That knows my grief, and by whate'er can move you, Relax a little your paternal rights, And free my love from this obedience! Oh, do not make me, by your harsh command, Complain to Heaven you ever were my father; Do not make wretched this poor life you gave me. If, crossing that fond hope which I had formed, You'll not permit me to belong to one Whom I have dared to love, at least, I beg you Upon my knees, oh, save me from the torment Of being possessed by one whom I abhor! And do not drive me to some desperate act By exercising all your rights upon me.

ORGON (a little touched) Come, come, my heart, be firm! no human weakness!

MARIANE I am not jealous of your love for him; Display it freely; give him your estate, And if that's not enough, add all of mine; I willingly agree, and give it up, If only you'll not give him me, your daughter; Oh, rather let a convent's rigid rule Wear out the wretched days that Heaven allots me.

ORGON These girls are ninnies!—always turning nuns When fathers thwart their silly love-affairs. Get on your feet! The more you hate to have him, The more 'twill help you earn your soul's salvation. So, mortify your senses by this marriage, And don't vex me about it any more.

DORINE But what ... ?

ORGON You hold your tongue, before your betters. Don't dare to say a single word, I tell you.

CLEANTE If you will let me answer, and advise ...

ORGON Brother, I value your advice most highly; 'Tis well thought out; no better can be had; But you'll allow me—not to follow it.

ELMIRE (to her husband) I can't find words to cope with such a case; Your blindness makes me quite astounded at you. You are bewitched with him, to disbelieve The things we tell you happened here to-day.

ORGON I am your humble servant, and can see Things, when they're plain as noses on folks' faces, I know you're partial to my rascal son, And didn't dare to disavow the trick He tried to play on this poor man; besides, You were too calm, to be believed; if that Had happened, you'd have been far more disturbed.

ELMIRE And must our honour always rush to arms At the mere mention of illicit love? Or can we answer no attack upon it Except with blazing eyes and lips of scorn? For my part, I just laugh away such nonsense; I've no desire to make a loud to-do. Our virtue should, I think, be gentle-natured; Nor can I quite approve those savage prudes Whose honour arms itself with teeth and claws To tear men's eyes out at the slightest word. Heaven preserve me from that kind of honour! I like my virtue not to be a vixen, And I believe a quiet cold rebuff No less effective to repulse a lover.

ORGON I know ... and you can't throw me off the scent.

ELMIRE Once more, I am astounded at your weakness; I wonder what your unbelief would answer, If I should let you see we've told the truth?

ORGON See it?

ELMIRE Yes.

ORGON Nonsense.

ELMIRE Come! If I should find A way to make you see it clear as day?

ORGON All rubbish.

ELMIRE What a man! But answer me. I'm not proposing now that you believe us; But let's suppose that here, from proper hiding, You should be made to see and hear all plainly; What would you say then, to your man of virtue?

ORGON Why, then, I'd say ... say nothing. It can't be.

ELMIRE Your error has endured too long already, And quite too long you've branded me a liar. I must at once, for my own satisfaction, Make you a witness of the things we've told you.

ORGON Amen! I take you at your word. We'll see What tricks you have, and how you'll keep your promise.

ELMIRE (to Dorine) Send him to me.

DORINE (to Elmire) The man's a crafty codger, Perhaps you'll find it difficult to catch him.

ELMIRE (to Dorine) Oh no! A lover's never hard to cheat, And self-conceit leads straight to self-deceit. Bid him come down to me.

(To Cleante and Mariane) And you, withdraw.

Scene 4

ELMIRE, ORGON

ELMIRE Bring up this table, and get under it.

ORGON What?

ELMIRE One essential is to hide you well.

ORGON Why under there?

ELMIRE Oh, dear! Do as I say; I know what I'm about, as you shall see. Get under, now, I tell you; and once there Be careful no one either sees or hears you.

ORGON I'm going a long way to humour you, I must say; but I'll see you through your scheme.

ELMIRE And then you'll have, I think, no more to say.

(To her husband, who is now under the table.) But mind, I'm going to meddle with strange matters; Prepare yourself to be in no wise shocked. Whatever I may say must pass, because 'Tis only to convince you, as I promised. By wheedling speeches, since I'm forced to do it, I'll make this hypocrite put off his mask, Flatter the longings of his shameless passion, And give free play to all his impudence. But, since 'tis for your sake, to prove to you His guilt, that I shall feign to share his love, I can leave off as soon as you're convinced, And things shall go no farther than you choose. So, when you think they've gone quite far enough, It is for you to stop his mad pursuit, To spare your wife, and not expose me farther Than you shall need, yourself, to undeceive you. It is your own affair, and you must end it When ... Here he comes. Keep still, don't show yourself.

Scene 5

TARTUFFE, ELMIRE; ORGON (under the table)

TARTUFFE They told me that you wished to see me here.

ELMIRE Yes. I have secrets for your ear alone. But shut the door first, and look everywhere For fear of spies.

(Tartuffe goes and closes the door, and comes back.) We surely can't afford Another scene like that we had just now; Was ever anyone so caught before! Damis did frighten me most terribly On your account; you saw I did my best To baffle his design, and calm his anger. But I was so confused, I never thought To contradict his story; still, thank Heaven, Things turned out all the better, as it happened, And now we're on an even safer footing. The high esteem you're held in, laid the storm; My husband can have no suspicion of you, And even insists, to spite the scandal-mongers, That we shall be together constantly; So that is how, without the risk of blame, I can be here locked up with you alone, And can reveal to you my heart, perhaps Only too ready to allow your passion.

TARTUFFE Your words are somewhat hard to understand, Madam; just now you used a different style.

ELMIRE If that refusal has offended you, How little do you know a woman's heart! How ill you guess what it would have you know, When it presents so feeble a defence! Always, at first, our modesty resists The tender feelings you inspire us with. Whatever cause we find to justify The love that masters us, we still must feel Some little shame in owning it; and strive To make as though we would not, when we would. But from the very way we go about it We let a lover know our heart surrenders, The while our lips, for honour's sake, oppose Our heart's desire, and in refusing promise. I'm telling you my secret all too freely And with too little heed to modesty. But—now that I've made bold to speak— pray tell me. Should I have tried to keep Damis from speaking, Should I have heard the offer of your heart So quietly, and suffered all your pleading, And taken it just as I did—remember— If such a declaration had not pleased me, And, when I tried my utmost to persuade you Not to accept the marriage that was talked of, What should my earnestness have hinted to you If not the interest that you've inspired, And my chagrin, should such a match compel me To share a heart I want all to myself?

TARTUFFE 'Tis, past a doubt, the height of happiness, To hear such words from lips we dote upon; Their honeyed sweetness pours through all my senses Long draughts of suavity ineffable. My heart employs its utmost zeal to please you, And counts your love its one beatitude; And yet that heart must beg that you allow it To doubt a little its felicity. I well might think these words an honest trick To make me break off this approaching marriage; And if I may express myself quite plainly, I cannot trust these too enchanting words Until the granting of some little favour I sigh for, shall assure me of their truth And build within my soul, on firm foundations, A lasting faith in your sweet charity.

ELMIRE (coughing to draw her husband's attention) What! Must you go so fast?—and all at once Exhaust the whole love of a woman's heart? She does herself the violence to make This dear confession of her love, and you Are not yet satisfied, and will not be Without the granting of her utmost favours?

TARTUFFE The less a blessing is deserved, the less We dare to hope for it; and words alone Can ill assuage our love's desires. A fate Too full of happiness, seems doubtful still; We must enjoy it ere we can believe it. And I, who know how little I deserve Your goodness, doubt the fortunes of my daring; So I shall trust to nothing, madam, till You have convinced my love by something real.

ELMIRE Ah! How your love enacts the tyrant's role, And throws my mind into a strange confusion! With what fierce sway it rules a conquered heart, And violently will have its wishes granted! What! Is there no escape from your pursuit? No respite even?—not a breathing space? Nay, is it decent to be so exacting, And so abuse by urgency the weakness You may discover in a woman's heart?

TARTUFFE But if my worship wins your gracious favour, Then why refuse me some sure proof thereof?

ELMIRE But how can I consent to what you wish, Without offending Heaven you talk so much of?

TARTUFFE If Heaven is all that stands now in my way, I'll easily remove that little hindrance; Your heart need not hold back for such a trifle.

ELMIRE But they affright us so with Heaven's commands!

TARTUFFE I can dispel these foolish fears, dear madam; I know the art of pacifying scruples Heaven forbids, 'tis true, some satisfactions; But we find means to make things right with Heaven.

('Tis a scoundrel speaking.) [5]

[Footnote 5: Moliere's note, in the original edition.]

There is a science, madam, that instructs us How to enlarge the limits of our conscience According to our various occasions, And rectify the evil of the deed According to our purity of motive. I'll duly teach you all these secrets, madam; You only need to let yourself be guided. Content my wishes, have no fear at all; I answer for't, and take the sin upon me.

(Elmire coughs still louder.) Your cough is very bad.

ELMIRE Yes, I'm in torture.

TARTUFFE Would you accept this bit of licorice?

ELMIRE The case is obstinate, I find; and all The licorice in the world will do no good.

TARTUFFE 'Tis very trying.

ELMIRE More than words can say.

TARTUFFE In any case, your scruple's easily Removed. With me you're sure of secrecy, And there's no harm unless a thing is known. The public scandal is what brings offence, And secret sinning is not sin at all.

ELMIRE (after coughing again) So then, I see I must resolve to yield; I must consent to grant you everything, And cannot hope to give full satisfaction Or win full confidence, at lesser cost. No doubt 'tis very hard to come to this; 'Tis quite against my will I go so far; But since I must be forced to it, since nothing That can be said suffices for belief, Since more convincing proof is still demanded, I must make up my mind to humour people. If my consent give reason for offence, So much the worse for him who forced me to it; The fault can surely not be counted mine.

TARTUFFE It need not, madam; and the thing itself ...

ELMIRE Open the door, I pray you, and just see Whether my husband's not there, in the hall.

TARTUFFE Why take such care for him? Between ourselves, He is a man to lead round by the nose. He's capable of glorying in our meetings; I've fooled him so, he'd see all, and deny it.

ELMIRE No matter; go, I beg you, look about, And carefully examine every corner.

Scene 6

ORGON, ELMIRE

ORGON (crawling out from under the table) That is, I own, a man ... abominable! I can't get over it; the whole thing floors me.

ELMIRE What? You come out so soon? You cannot mean it! Get back under the table; 'tis not time yet; Wait till the end, to see, and make quite certain, And don't believe a thing on mere conjecture.

ORGON Nothing more wicked e'er came out of Hell.

ELMIRE Dear me! Don't go and credit things too lightly. No, let yourself be thoroughly convinced; Don't yield too soon, for fear you'll be mistaken.

(As Tartuffe enters, she makes her husband stand behind her.)

Scene 7

TARTUFFE, ELMIRE, ORGON

TARTUFFE (not seeing Orgon) All things conspire toward my satisfaction, Madam, I've searched the whole apartment through. There's no one here; and now my ravished soul ...

ORGON (stopping him) Softly! You are too eager in your amours; You needn't be so passionate. Ah ha! My holy man! You want to put it on me! How is your soul abandoned to temptation! Marry my daughter, eh?—and want my wife, too? I doubted long enough if this was earnest, Expecting all the time the tone would change; But now the proof's been carried far enough; I'm satisfied, and ask no more, for my part.

ELMIRE (to Tartuffe) 'Twas quite against my character to play This part; but I was forced to treat you so.

TARTUFFE What? You believe ... ?

ORGON Come, now, no protestations. Get out from here, and make no fuss about it.

TARTUFFE But my intent ...

ORGON That talk is out of season. You leave my house this instant.

TARTUFFE You're the one To leave it, you who play the master here! This house belongs to me, I'll have you know, And show you plainly it's no use to turn To these low tricks, to pick a quarrel with me, And that you can't insult me at your pleasure, For I have wherewith to confound your lies, Avenge offended Heaven, and compel Those to repent who talk to me of leaving.

Scene 8

ELMIRE, ORGON

ELMIRE What sort of speech is this? What can it mean?

ORGON My faith, I'm dazed. This is no laughing matter.

ELMIRE What?

ORGON From his words I see my great mistake; The deed of gift is one thing troubles me.

ELMIRE The deed of gift ...

ORGON Yes, that is past recall. But I've another thing to make me anxious.

ELMIRE What's that?

ORGON You shall know all. Let's see at once Whether a certain box is still upstairs.

Act 5

Scene 1

ORGON, CLEANTE

CLEANTE Whither away so fast?

ORGON How should I know?

CLEANTE Methinks we should begin by taking counsel To see what can be done to meet the case.

ORGON I'm all worked up about that wretched box. More than all else it drives me to despair.

CLEANTE That box must hide some mighty mystery?

ORGON Argas, my friend who is in trouble, brought it Himself, most secretly, and left it with me. He chose me, in his exile, for this trust; And on these documents, from what he said, I judge his life and property depend.

CLEANTE How could you trust them to another's hands?

ORGON By reason of a conscientious scruple. I went straight to my traitor, to confide In him; his sophistry made me believe That I must give the box to him to keep, So that, in case of search, I might deny My having it at all, and still, by favour Of this evasion, keep my conscience clear Even in taking oath against the truth.

CLEANTE Your case is bad, so far as I can see; This deed of gift, this trusting of the secret To him, were both—to state my frank opinion— Steps that you took too lightly; he can lead you To any length, with these for hostages; And since he holds you at such disadvantage, You'd be still more imprudent, to provoke him; So you must go some gentler way about.

ORGON What! Can a soul so base, a heart so false, Hide neath the semblance of such touching fervour? I took him in, a vagabond, a beggar! ... 'Tis too much! No more pious folk for me! I shall abhor them utterly forever, And henceforth treat them worse than any devil.

CLEANTE So! There you go again, quite off the handle! In nothing do you keep an even temper. You never know what reason is, but always Jump first to one extreme, and then the other. You see your error, and you recognise That you've been cozened by a feigned zeal; But to make up for't, in the name of reason, Why should you plunge into a worse mistake, And find no difference in character Between a worthless scamp, and all good people? What! Just because a rascal boldly duped you With pompous show of false austerity, Must you needs have it everybody's like him, And no one's truly pious nowadays? Leave such conclusions to mere infidels; Distinguish virtue from its counterfeit, Don't give esteem too quickly, at a venture, But try to keep, in this, the golden mean. If you can help it, don't uphold imposture; But do not rail at true devoutness, either; And if you must fall into one extreme, Then rather err again the other way.

Scene 2

DAMIS, ORGON, CLEANTE

DAMIS What! father, can the scoundrel threaten you, Forget the many benefits received, And in his base abominable pride Make of your very favours arms against you?

ORGON Too true, my son. It tortures me to think on't.

DAMIS Let me alone, I'll chop his ears off for him. We must deal roundly with his insolence; 'Tis I must free you from him at a blow; 'Tis I, to set things right, must strike him down.

CLEANTE Spoke like a true young man. Now just calm down, And moderate your towering tantrums, will you? We live in such an age, with such a king, That violence can not advance our cause.

Scene 3

MADAME PERNELLE, ORGON, ELMIRE, CLEANTE, MARIANE, DAMIS, DORINE

MADAME PERNELLE What's this? I hear of fearful mysteries!

ORGON Strange things indeed, for my own eyes to witness; You see how I'm requited for my kindness, I zealously receive a wretched beggar, I lodge him, entertain him like my brother, Load him with benefactions every day, Give him my daughter, give him all my fortune: And he meanwhile, the villain, rascal, wretch, Tries with black treason to suborn my wife, And not content with such a foul design, He dares to menace me with my own favours, And would make use of those advantages Which my too foolish kindness armed him with, To ruin me, to take my fortune from me, And leave me in the state I saved him from.

DORINE Poor man!

MADAME PERNELLE My son, I cannot possibly Believe he could intend so black a deed.

ORGON What?

MADAME PERNELLE Worthy men are still the sport of envy.

ORGON Mother, what do you mean by such a speech?

MADAME PERNELLE There are strange goings-on about your house, And everybody knows your people hate him.

ORGON What's that to do with what I tell you now?

MADAME PERNELLE I always said, my son, when you were little: That virtue here below is hated ever; The envious may die, but envy never.

78

ORGON What's that fine speech to do with present facts?

MADAME PERNELLE Be sure, they've forged a hundred silly lies ...

ORGON I've told you once, I saw it all myself.

MADAME PERNELLE For slanderers abound in calumnies ...

ORGON Mother, you'd make me damn my soul. I tell you I saw with my own eyes his shamelessness.

MADAME PERNELLE Their tongues for spitting venom never lack, There's nothing here below they'll not attack.

ORGON Your speech has not a single grain of sense. I saw it, harkee, saw it, with these eyes I saw—d'ye know what saw means?—must I say it A hundred times, and din it in your ears?

MADAME PERNELLE My dear, appearances are oft deceiving, And seeing shouldn't always be believing.

ORGON I'll go mad.

MADAME PERNELLE False suspicions may delude, And good to evil oft is misconstrued.

ORGON Must I construe as Christian charity The wish to kiss my wife!

MADAME PERNELLE You must, at least, Have just foundation for accusing people, And wait until you see a thing for sure.

ORGON The devil! How could I see any surer? Should I have waited till, before my eyes, He ... No, you'll make me say things quite improper.

MADAME PERNELLE In short, 'tis known too pure a zeal inflames him; And so, I cannot possibly conceive That he should try to do what's charged against him.

ORGON If you were not my mother, I should say Such things! ... I know not what, I'm so enraged!

DORINE (to Orgon) Fortune has paid you fair, to be so doubted; You flouted our report, now yours is flouted.

CLEANTE We're wasting time here in the merest trifling, Which we should rather use in taking measures To guard ourselves against the scoundrel's threats.

DAMIS You think his impudence could go far?

ELMIRE For one, I can't believe it possible; Why, his ingratitude would be too patent.

CLEANTE Don't trust to that; he'll find abundant warrant To give good colour to his acts against you; And for less cause than this, a strong cabal Can make one's life a labyrinth of troubles. I tell you once again: armed as he is You never should have pushed him quite so far.

ORGON True; yet what could I do? The rascal's pride Made me lose all control of my resentment.

CLEANTE I wish with all my heart that some pretence Of peace could be patched up between you two

ELMIRE If I had known what weapons he was armed with, I never should have raised such an alarm, And my ...

ORGON (to Dorine, seeing Mr. Loyal come in) Who's coming now? Go quick, find out. I'm in a fine state to receive a visit!

Scene 4

ORGON, MADAME PERNELLE, ELMIRE, MARIANE, CLEANTE, DAMIS, DORINE, MR. LOYAL

MR. LOYAL (to Dorine, at the back of the stage) Good day, good sister. Pray you, let me see The master of the house.

DORINE He's occupied; I think he can see nobody at present.

MR. LOYAL I'm not by way of being unwelcome here. My coming can, I think, nowise displease him; My errand will be found to his advantage.

DORINE Your name, then?

MR. LOYAL Tell him simply that his friend Mr. Tartuffe has sent me, for his goods ...

DORINE (to Orgon) It is a man who comes, with civil manners, Sent by Tartuffe, he says, upon an errand That you'll be pleased with.

CLEANTE (to Orgon) Surely you must see him, And find out who he is, and what he wants.

ORGON (to Cleante) Perhaps he's come to make it up between us: How shall I treat him?

CLEANTE You must not get angry; And if he talks of reconciliation Accept it.

MR. LOYAL (to Orgon) Sir, good-day. And Heaven send Harm to your enemies, favour to you.

ORGON (aside to Cleante) This mild beginning suits with my conjectures And promises some compromise already.

MR. LOYAL All of your house has long been dear to me; I had the honour, sir, to serve your father.

ORGON Sir, I am much ashamed, and ask your pardon For not recalling now your face or name.

MR. LOYAL My name is Loyal. I'm from Normandy. My office is court-bailiff, in despite Of envy; and for forty years, thank Heaven, It's been my fortune to perform that office With honour. So I've come, sir, by your leave To render service of a certain writ ...

ORGON What, you are here to ...

MR. LOYAL Pray, sir, don't be angry. 'Tis nothing, sir, but just a little summons:— Order to vacate, you and yours, this house, Move out your furniture, make room for others, And that without delay or putting off, As needs must be ...

ORGON I? Leave this house?

MR. LOYAL Yes, please, sir The house is now, as you well know, of course, Mr. Tartuffe's. And he, beyond dispute, Of all your goods is henceforth lord and master By virtue of a contract here attached, Drawn in due form, and unassailable.

DAMIS (to Mr. Loyal) Your insolence is monstrous, and astounding!

MR. LOYAL (to Damis) I have no business, sir, that touches you;

(Pointing to Orgon) This is the gentleman. He's fair and courteous, And knows too well a gentleman's behaviour To wish in any wise to question justice.

ORGON But ...

MR. LOYAL Sir, I know you would not for a million Wish to rebel; like a good citizen You'll let me put in force the court's decree.

DAMIS Your long black gown may well, before you know it, Mister Court-bailiff, get a thorough beating.

MR. LOYAL (to Orgon) Sir, make your son be silent or withdraw. I should be loath to have to set things down, And see your names inscribed in my report.

DORINE (aside) This Mr. Loyal's looks are most disloyal.

MR. LOYAL I have much feeling for respectable And honest folk like you, sir, and consented To serve these papers, only to oblige you, And thus prevent the choice of any other Who, less possessed of zeal for you than I am Might order matters in less gentle fashion.

ORGON And how could one do worse than order people Out of their house?

MR. LOYAL Why, we allow you time; And even will suspend until to-morrow The execution of the order, sir. I'll merely, without scandal, quietly, Come here and spend the night, with half a score Of officers; and just for form's sake, please, You'll bring your keys to me, before retiring. I will take care not to disturb your rest, And see there's no unseemly conduct here. But by to-morrow, and at early morning, You must make haste to move your least belongings; My men will help you—I have chosen strong ones To serve you, sir, in clearing out the house. No one could act more generously, I fancy, And, since I'm treating you with great indulgence, I beg you'll do as well by me, and see I'm not disturbed in my discharge of duty.

ORGON I'd give this very minute, and not grudge it, The hundred best gold louis I have left, If I could just indulge myself, and land My fist, for one good square one, on his snout.

CLEANTE (aside to Orgon) Careful!—don't make things worse.

DAMIS Such insolence! I hardly can restrain myself. My hands Are itching to be at him.

DORINE By my faith, With such a fine broad back, good Mr. Loyal, A little beating would become you well.

MR. LOYAL My girl, such infamous words are actionable. And warrants can be issued against women.

83

CLEANTE (to Mr. Loyal) Enough of this discussion, sir; have done. Give us the paper, and then leave us, pray.

MR. LOYAL Then au revoir. Heaven keep you from disaster!

ORGON May Heaven confound you both, you and your master!

Scene 5

ORGON, MADAME PERNELLE, ELMIRE, CLEANTE, MARIANE, DAMIS, DORINE

ORGON Well, mother, am I right or am I not? This writ may help you now to judge the matter. Or don't you see his treason even yet?

MADAME PERNELLE I'm all amazed, befuddled, and beflustered!

DORINE (to Orgon) You are quite wrong, you have no right to blame him; This action only proves his good intentions. Love for his neighbour makes his virtue perfect; And knowing money is a root of evil, In Christian charity, he'd take away Whatever things may hinder your salvation.

ORGON Be still. You always need to have that told you.

CLEANTE (to Orgon) Come, let us see what course you are to follow.

ELMIRE Go and expose his bold ingratitude. Such action must invalidate the contract; His perfidy must now appear too black To bring him the success that he expects.

Scene 6

VALERE, ORGON, MADAME PERNELLE, ELMIRE, CLEANTE, MARIANE, DAMIS, DORINE

VALERE 'Tis with regret, sir, that I bring bad news; But urgent danger forces me to do so. A close and intimate friend of mine, who knows The interest I take in what concerns you, Has gone so far, for my sake, as to break The secrecy that's due to state affairs, And sent me word but now, that leaves you only The one expedient of sudden flight. The villain who so long imposed upon you, Found means, an hour ago, to see the prince, And to accuse you (among other things) By putting in his hands the private strong-box Of a state-criminal, whose guilty secret, You, failing in your duty as a subject, (He says) have kept. I know no more of it Save that a warrant's drawn against you, sir, And for the greater surety, that same rascal Comes with the officer who must arrest you.

CLEANTE His rights are armed; and this is how the scoundrel Seeks to secure the property he claims.

ORGON Man is a wicked animal, I'll own it!

VALERE The least delay may still be fatal, sir. I have my carriage, and a thousand louis, Provided for your journey, at the door. Let's lose no time; the bolt is swift to strike, And such as only flight can save you from. I'll be your guide to seek a place of safety, And stay with you until you reach it, sir.

ORGON How much I owe to your obliging care! Another time must serve to thank you fitly; And I pray Heaven to grant me so much favour That I may some day recompense your service. Good-bye; see to it, all of you ...

CLEANTE Come hurry; We'll see to everything that's needful, brother.

Scene 7

TARTUFFE, AN OFFICER, MADAME PERNELLE, ORGON, ELMIRE, CLEANTE, MARIANE, VALERE, DAMIS, DORINE

TARTUFFE (stopping Orgon) Softly, sir, softly; do not run so fast; You haven't far to go to find your lodging; By order of the prince, we here arrest you.

ORGON Traitor! You saved this worst stroke for the last; This crowns your perfidies, and ruins me.

TARTUFFE I shall not be embittered by your insults, For Heaven has taught me to endure all things.

CLEANTE Your moderation, I must own, is great.

DAMIS How shamelessly the wretch makes bold with Heaven!

TARTUFFE Your ravings cannot move me; all my thought Is but to do my duty.

MARIANE You must claim Great glory from this honourable act.

TARTUFFE The act cannot be aught but honourable, Coming from that high power which sends me here.

ORGON Ungrateful wretch, do you forget 'twas I That rescued you from utter misery?

TARTUFFE I've not forgot some help you may have given; But my first duty now is toward my prince. The higher power of that most sacred claim Must stifle in my heart all gratitude; And to such puissant ties I'd sacrifice My friend, my wife, my kindred, and myself.

ELMIRE The hypocrite!

DORINE How well he knows the trick Of cloaking him with what we most revere!

CLEANTE But if the motive that you make parade of Is perfect as you say, why should it wait To show itself, until the day he caught you Soliciting his wife? How happens it You have not thought to go inform against him Until his honour forces him to drive you Out of his house? And though I need not mention That he'd just given you his whole estate, Still, if you meant to treat him now as guilty, How could you then consent to take his gift?

TARTUFFE (to the Officer) Pray, sir, deliver me from all this clamour; Be good enough to carry out your order.

THE OFFICER Yes, I've too long delayed its execution; 'Tis very fitting you should urge me to it; So therefore, you must follow me at once To prison, where you'll find your lodging ready.

TARTUFFE Who? I, sir?

THE OFFICER You.

TARTUFFE By why to prison?

THE OFFICER You Are not the one to whom I owe account. You, sir (to Orgon), recover from your hot alarm. Our prince is not a friend to double dealing, His eyes can read men's inmost hearts, and all The art of hypocrites cannot deceive him. His sharp discernment sees things clear and true; His mind cannot too easily be swayed, For reason always holds the balance even. He honours and exalts true piety, But knows the false, and views it with disgust. This fellow was by no means apt to fool him, Far subtler snares have failed against his wisdom, And his quick insight pierced immediately The hidden baseness of this tortuous heart. Accusing you, the knave betrayed himself, And by true recompense of Heaven's justice He stood revealed before our monarch's eyes A scoundrel known before by other names, Whose horrid crimes, detailed at length, might fill A long-drawn history of many volumes. Our monarch—to resolve you in a word— Detesting his ingratitude and baseness, Added this horror to his other crimes, And sent me hither under his direction To see his insolence out-top itself, And force him then to give you satisfaction. Your papers, which the traitor says are his, I am to take from him, and give you back; The deed of gift transferring your estate Our monarch's sovereign will makes null and void; And for the secret personal offence Your friend involved you in, he pardons you: Thus he rewards your recent zeal, displayed In helping to maintain his rights, and shows How well his heart, when it is least expected, Knows how to recompense a noble deed, And will not let true merit miss its due, Remembering always rather good than evil.

DORINE Now Heaven be praised!

MADAME PERNELLE At last I breathe again.

ELMIRE A happy outcome!

MARIANE Who'd have dared to hope it?

ORGON (to Tartuffe, who is being led by the officer) There traitor! Now you're ...

Scene 8

MADAME PERNELLE, ORGON, ELMIRE, MARIANE, CLEANTE, VALERE, DAMIS, DORINE

CLEANTE Brother, hold!—and don't Descend to such indignities, I beg you. Leave the poor wretch to his unhappy fate, And let remorse oppress him, but not you. Hope rather that his heart may now return To virtue, hate his vice, reform his ways, And win the pardon of our glorious prince; While you must straightway go, and on your knees Repay with thanks his noble generous kindness.

ORGON Well said! We'll go, and at his feet kneel down, With joy to thank him for his goodness shown; And this first duty done, with honours due, We'll then attend upon another, too. With wedded happiness reward Valere, And crown a lover noble and sincere.

15285791R00052

Made in the USA
Middletown, DE
30 October 2014